M000158830

(untitled) 1991

The Photography of

JOHN BRILL

Text by

Leah Ollman

ISBN: 1 - 878607-79-0

First Edition: 2500 copies

Book Design by Aude Choimet

Typeset in Garamond

Printed in Hong Kong

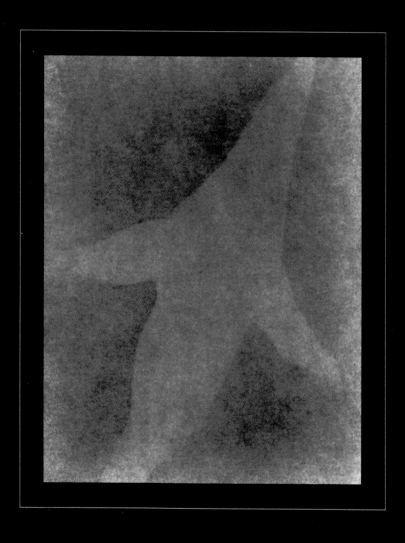

Figment of My Imagination 1992

Helen, Passaic, NJ 1985

Believe

Believe everything you've heard about those two, photography and time. The rumors, the theories, even the lies—they're all true. Shameless seducers, both of them. Their cunning liaison ensnares us all, compelling us to remember, betraying us into forgetting.

Theirs is a bond built of contradiction, convincing contradiction. Does photography slow time or freeze it? Devour it or honor it? Succumb to it or defy it? Does photography embalm time or revivify it? Clarify it or unravel its logic? Stretch it or compress it? All of these, and at once. The photograph—like time, like memory—is a swarm of mixed messages. About all that can be said conclusively is that photographs disrupt time's conventionally perceived flow.

"Time is the substance from which I am made.
Time is a river which carries me along, but I am the river;
it is the tiger that devours me, but I am the tiger;
it is a fire that consumes me, but I am the fire."

--Jorge Luis Borges (1)

Family Holiday Album #13 1990

Family Holiday Album #14 1990

Family Holiday Album #15 1990

Family Holiday Album #19 1990

Family Holiday Album #25 1990

Self-portrait, Lodi, NJ 1987

Wonders and lures

Since its invention in 1839, photography has manifested the desire to affirm and to frame the visible world, but for nearly as long, it's also been the vehicle for another desire: to capture the unseen. Psychography—writing by the soul or psychic power—and spirit photography emerged as early as the 1850s as pseudo-scientific, earnest quests into the further reaches of photography's capacity. Photography is a *medium*, after all. A go-between. It serves the quest for knowledge as readily as it serves the irrepressible urge for deception. It depends who's using it, and it depends what we're expecting it to produce. Just what do we think a material image of the immaterial might look like?

In the 1930s, a husband-and-wife team of electrical experts in Russia claimed to have photographed auras, the energy fields surrounding living things. The discovery was made accidentally, after the husband received an electrical shock at work, then returned home to help his wife with some photographic processing. The film he made contact with registered unexpected colors. Rumor spread that the couple, named Kirlian, had photographed the soul.

Kirlian photographs—made by introducing a subject to electrical charge—were said to show how the aura varied according to the changing emotional or physical state of a subject. Pathological conditions, it was claimed, revealed themselves in these photographs even before a subject presented any outward symptoms. Researchers made Kirlian photographs of healers' hands to document their privileged level of energy and to record its transfer in the act of healing.

Stuntman, trickster

Sitting in a generic hotel room in an American city in the early 1960s, Ted Serios stared into the lens of a Polaroid camera and made a picture. In a university lab, in a researcher's living room, in a tv studio, he made others.

Rarely did the photographs accurately capture him or his surroundings at the time. Instead they showed other landscapes—structures in Russia, France, Chicago, the sign over a hotel no longer in existence. Blurred and usually tilted, the views often resonated with whatever Serios had been concentrating on when the shutter clicked. These were photographs of his thoughts.

Or so he claimed.

Serios drank heavily before and during his photo sessions. His pulse accelerated. He entered a trance-like state. Afterward, he coughed blood. His "thoughtographs," aggressively championed by a professor of psychiatry at the University of Colorado Medical School, became a minor rage, and Serios, otherwise unemployed, appeared on magazine covers and television shows. His ability to produce a global range of photographs from wherever he sat became a rallying cry for parapsychologists. Finally, they exclaimed, the power of mind over matter has been demonstrated, visualized, legitimized.

Brill was a teenager in the mid-'60s when he saw one of Serios' tv appearances. For years already, since the age of eight, he had been "absolutely consumed by the act of capturing slices of space-time with a camera." When Serios came on, he was skeptical—and entranced: "Looking at the tiny image of a comical, alcoholic snake oil salesman on my little black and white tv, I may as well have been watching god descend into my living room."

Brill earned a degree in physiological psychology, steeping himself in the scientific method—the practice of discriminating fact from hypothesis—before committing himself in 1981 to art-making. Beginning with staged portraits and self-portraits, his imagery became increasingly nebulous, reflecting his interest "in how resonance could remain unaffected by the systematic removal of content." Toward the end of the '80s, he began seriously toying with the idea of the "thoughtograph." He scavenged for pictures, made some from life and others from the television screen, then worked to distance the images from their origins through multiple printings, fragmentation, tonal shifts and value reversals. In the end, the pictures derive more from mind than from matter. They're

Self-portrait, Weehawken, NJ 1987

projections of his will, contrived out of pure desire. Physical representations of the incorporeal.

"There's an implicit yearning in all of us to be shown evidence of our thoughts, our memories, a world beyond our normal senses," Brill says. "To photograph that which can't be photographed." What if we could photograph a memory, a "spirit," or a fleeting thought? What would such a picture look like?

Self-portrait, Union City, NJ 1987

Self-portrait, Newark, NJ 1987

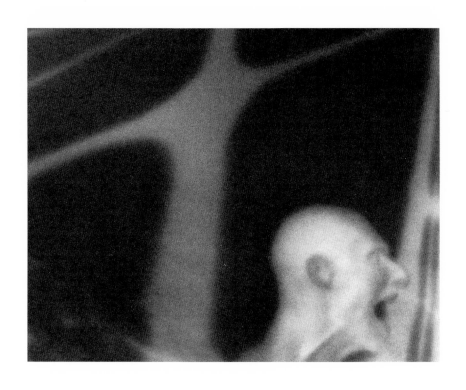

Self-portrait, Paterson, NJ 1987

Portrait #2 1991

Engrams

As defined in the Concise Oxford Dictionary, an engram is not only an amorphous thing, but a dubious one as well: "memory-trace, supposed permanent change in brain accounting for existence of memory."

Brill's series of photographs collectively titled *Engrams* (1991-93) consists of mostly small images, variably toned, invariably blurred. Faces and figures recur but distilled, distended, erased of particularities, shrunken in a corner, faded in the distance, as wisps of silhouettes, pools of shadow. He sizes his prints like old snapshots, personal artifacts, bordering them with that familiar, thin frame of white. He vignettes the corners and some-times tilts the angle, forging a casualness, a "best-that-conditions-would-allow ingenuousness" that lends the pictures homegrown authenticity. As a group, they resemble a disheveled catalog of elusive memories, or as Brill describes it, "the bedroom dresser/wall that you view in somebody else's dream."

Throughout its written history, memory has been conceived as something of a diasporic wanderer. Speculation over its true home, its native soil, has been rich and probing, yielding diverse hypotheses that have located memory first in the body and then in the mind. It was once believed that memory corresponded to the amount of light and dark in the body. When its position in the mind, as a cerebral function (however much we may experience it physically) became generally accepted, philosophers, writers and scientists envisioned memory as a "large and boundless chamber," a receptacle, a palace "with rooms beyond number," a library, a warehouse. Passive vessels all, they were believed to house memories the way shelves in the basement stored jars of tomatoes put up for the winter. The jar pulled down from the shelf in December was presumed to be the very same as the one put there in July, filled with the same fruit held in suspended ripeness.

Neutrality and consistency no longer anchor our modern conception of memory. Mnemosyne, it turns out, is a far more fickle goddess than the one whom ancient Greeks worshipped, back when remembering was crucial to social and physical survival. Now we have machines to store our data, and memory is accepted as a fallible, subjective process, governed by present needs more than past realities. Today, memory is valued less as the seat of knowledge than as a portal to our personal and cultural identities. Memory, in Proust's seductive view, connects us to our previous selves, which can be both affirming and disorienting. Either way, it cracks the monotony of expectation and habit, introducing a rich dissonance into the everyday.

Brill's hazy images pull us back, too, in their vague, entrancing way. They beckon us toward the previous, the slow, and the unseen, all attributes that have limited currency in our future-oriented, speed-loving culture, where what can't be counted, doesn't count. Brill's images look like photographs and work like memories. Or...they look like memories and work like photographs.

Portrait #3 1991

Portrait #11 1991

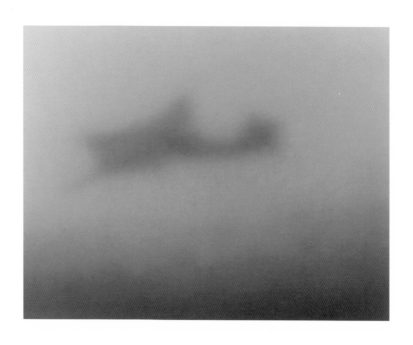

My First Airplane Ride 1992

(untitled) 1993

(untitled) 1992

(untitled) 1993

(untitled) 1991

Ennui #26 1994-97

Trusting doubt, doubting trust

Leaps of faith, Brill's photographs offer little information to gain traction on. Stripped of specificity and untethered from their sources in the physical world, the images are stranded in both time and space. Fragments, shadows, traces, whispers, all defiantly vague. Brill empties out and pares down, savoring the singular shape or pattern of contrast, and reveling in the process of creating a photograph by hand, out of sheer expectation, curiosity and will.

Ennui (1994-97) has even less of what would conventionally be called content than *Engrams*, the series that preceded it. It's an entire body of work, Brill says, "comprising pictures of nothing in particular." The suggestion of a hill, a tree, an airplane, a sailboat, a horizon, a pair of clouds, an accretion of shadow, an expanse of light. The images function, he says, as "minimalist Rorschachs," open to our projections, our own psychic, mnemonic baggage.

Brill may have released his photographs from their indexical relationship to the real, but still there to contend with is our assumption that such a relationship exists, fundamental to the photographic image. That expectation, if anything, is the subject of Brill's photographs. He engages it directly, either exploiting it or subverting it according to his own playfully deviant means.

His photographs are wholly fabricated. As Brill notes of his most recent series, *Reliquary*, the photographs are "souvenirs from an imaginary space—evidentiary documents from an illusory landscape on the periphery of consciousness. Physical manifestations of the innately impalpable exploration of mind, they include fleeting, half-seen glimpses of nonexistent beings, vicarious experience of conjectural phenomena, memories of events that never happened."

That indexical relationship, that presumed correspondence between photograph and material reality causes a certain trust to kick in automatically, and Brill betrays it—not maliciously, but generously, to expose the fallacies that the misplaced trust is built upon, to shake the rickety scaffolding of photographic veracity. The ephemeral, velvety beauty of Brill's pictures seduces us into embracing ambiguity and contradiction as valued qualities in themselves, and not just byproducts of certainty's absence.

If every photograph is a compact lesson, a document—from the Latin *docere*, to teach—Brill's teach us how little we truly know, and how much we leave to the silent mechanisms of faith, to the shorthand workings of perception and to the deep, murky wells of memory.

"Try to remember this: what you project
Is what you will perceive; what you perceive
With any passion, be it love or terror,
May take on whims and powers of its own."

--Richard Wilbur (2)

Ennui #2 1994-97

Ennui #3 1994-97

Ennui #5 1994-97

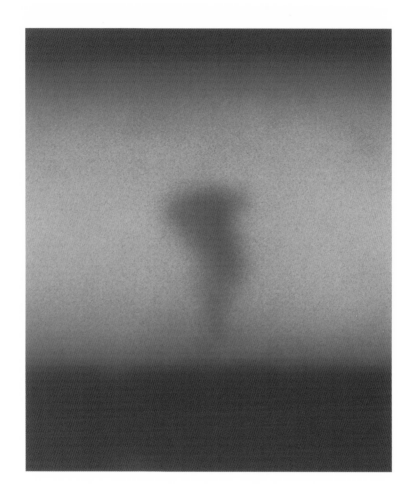

Ennui #7 1994-97

Ennui #9 1994-97

Ennui #19 1994-97

Ennui #21 1994-97

Ennui #25 1994-97

Ennui #34 1994-97

Ennui #48 1994-97

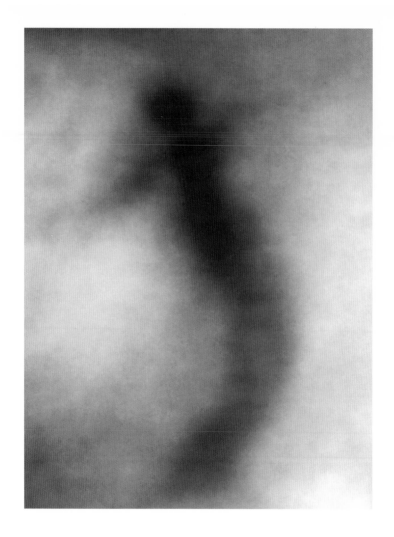

Discarnate 1999

The fact of fiction

B rill's photographs are as true as any, and as false. Some of the contradictions they thrive on are basic to the medium—for instance, the photograph's presentation of an absent subject, the preserved life it gives to the dead. Polarities conflate in the photographic image under any circumstances; what Brill does is spotlight that twisting dance of differences that reconciles itself on the page. Presence and absence, the authentic and the contrived, the abstract and the representational, the new and the old are among the mixed marriages consummated under Brill's watch.

His pictures, on first impression, do seem old, visions of memories dredged from a hazy past, and possibly relics themselves of an earlier era. Their sepia, steely purple and charcoal tones recall prints made from paper negatives in the first decades of photography. Brill resuscitates that process, the calotype, patented by William Henry Fox Talbot in 1841. The first negative/positive photographic process, calotypy delivered a clear but not utterly crisp image, and was largely replaced in 1851 by glass plate negatives coated with wet collodion, a method allowing greater articulation of detail. After 1851, only those photographers who preferred a more diffuse effect for artistic reasons continued to use paper negatives; the calotype had become functionally obsolete within a mere dozen years. Compared to the sharpness of the wet collodion negative and the mirror acuity of Daguerreotypes, calotypes were, according to one of Talbot's accomplices, "vague, foggy things."

Vague, foggy things are just what Brill aspires to make. He may begin with a clear, descriptive image, but through bleaching, drawing with graphite, burning and dodging, he degrades it, compromising its clarity. In his work, the paper negative acts, he says, as a matrix for all that follows. A variety of manipulations, "interventions," collectively transform the image, removing information so that the picture no longer tells but suggests, implies, promises, beckons.

In resuscitating a 19th-century process, Brill also revives an earlier state of wonder surrounding what Talbot called the "natural magic" of photography. He restores some of the mystery that surrounded photography at its inception, the feeling that it's rapturous and devious, emotionally, scientifically and spiritually powerful. Like other contemporary artists using obsolete photographic processes—Lyle Rexer terms them the "Antiquarian avant-garde"—Brill's methods come freighted with associations derived from 19th-century attitudes and uses of photography. Brill's work reminds us that photography began and remains a hybrid of magic, science and art. One British reporter exclaimed in 1839 that the invention "seems more like some marvel of a fairy tale or delusion of necromancy than a practical reality....The thing seems incredible, and, but for indisputable evidence, we should not at first hearing believe it; it is, however, a fact." (3)

Magic has barely a cranny to squeeze into between the cynicism and irony crowding the landscape of contemporary art. But Brill invests what might be dismissed as magic's quaintness with a sophisticated, self-conscious criticality. His is essentially a conceptual project, a cunning proliferation of purposeful fibs, executed with heartening sensuality and infused with romanticism. Brill is disarmingly honest in his role as impostor. He's after a seamless illusion that leaves the audience baffled, but hopes that we're also provoked into rooting out the truth—that photographic fact is factitious, that fiction deserves our trust, and trust, our doubt.

"...The world's
a dream, Basho said,
Not because that dream's
A falsehood, but because it's
Truer than it seems."

--Richard Wilbur (4)

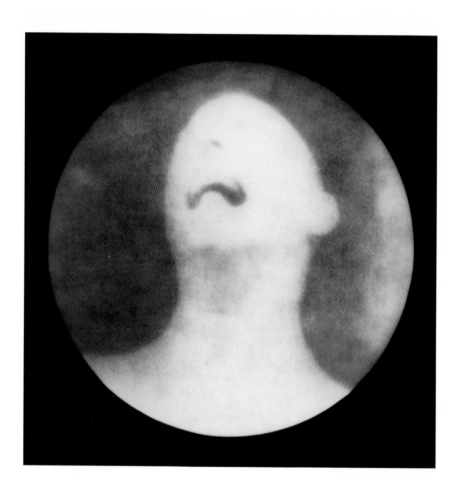

Rapture 1999

Visitation 2000

Ephemeron 1999

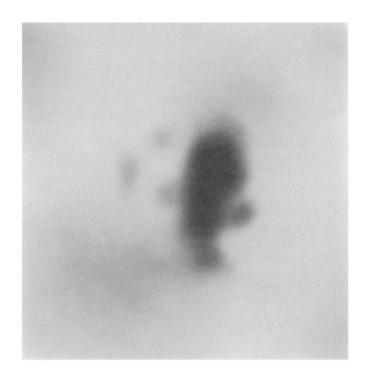

Little Gasping Head 2000

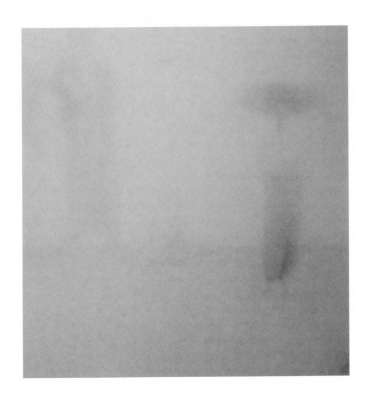

Chinese Spirit Photo 1999

Recurring Apparitions (Civil War battlefield, Alexandria, VA) 1999

Reccuring Apparition (India, 1960s) 1999

Dead 2000

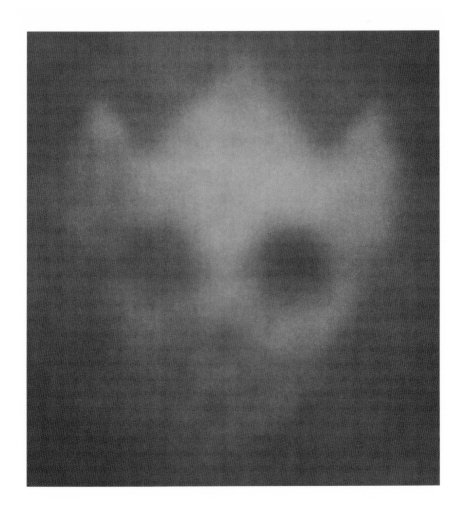

Vestige 1999

Residue 1999

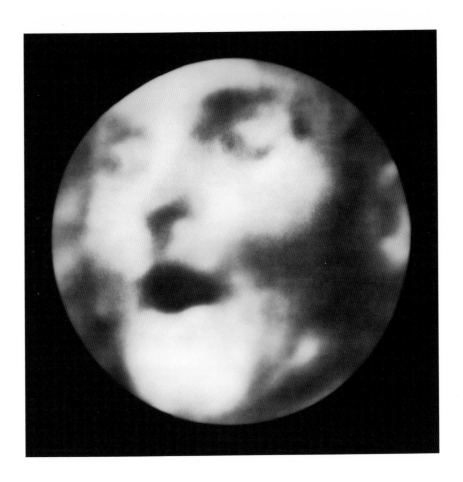

Ecstasis 1999

Portrait #14 1991

Unfixing the image

It's a shame that photography's inventors ever adopted the term *fixing the image* to describe the process of decreasing a print's sensitivity to light. Fixity implies inertness, sameness, and photographs don't work that way. They oscillate, fluctuate, waver between absence and presence, memory and expectation. They aren't stable entities filling the vault of visual possibility any more than memories are static deposits in a mental archive. Both photography and memory are fluid things, shifting and adapting according to the needs brought to them.

Brill's work flaunts its ambiguity but speaks in mellifluous, emotional truths. It skimps on resolution to better set in motion a collaborative process between maker and viewer. Incompleteness is part of the allure, for it forces us to fill in, to project, to extend, to draw upon both conditioned responses and personal associations. Photography as portal to negotiate the imagined, rather than as souvenir of the already witnessed.

No matter where photographs derive from, they all—not just Brill's—belong to a parallel, fictive reality. And they possess an exquisite authority, whether justly deserved or not. Photographs help us see through time, while time gives us the vocabulary to comprehend photographs.

Hold on, the image whispers. Let go.

"Time is mainly pictures,
After a while is only pictures."

--Reynolds Price (5)

Family Holiday Album #17 1990

NOTES:

1. Jorge Luis Borges, "A New Refutation of Time," in *Labyrinths: Selected Stories & Other Writings*, New York: New Directions, 1962, p.234.

2. Richard Wilbur, "Walking to Sleep," in *New and Collected Poems,* San Diego, New York, and London: Harcourt Brace & Company, 1988, p.158.

3. Beaumont Newhall, "Eighteen Thirty-Nine: The Birth of Photography," in *Photography: Discovery and Invention*, Malibu: J.Paul Getty Museum, 1990, p.22.

4. Wilbur, "Thyme Flowering among Rocks," in *New and Collected Poems*, p.143.

5. Reynolds Price, "Farewell with Photographs," in *The Collected Poems*, New York: Scribner, 1997, p.345.

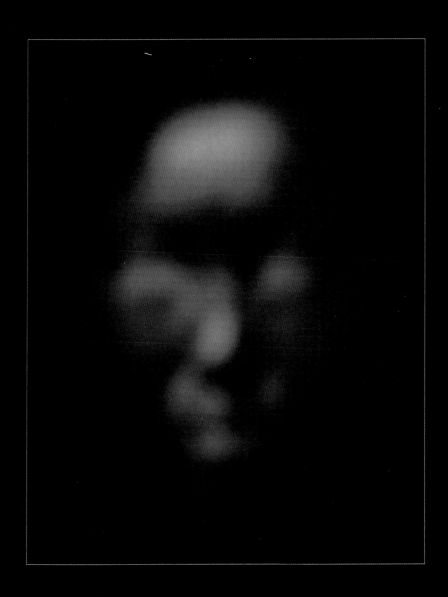

Trance 1999